The inner workings of an unkept mind

Justin Armstrong

BookLeaf
Publishing

India | USA | UK

Presentation by *BookLeaf Publishing*

Web: www.bookleafpub.com

E-mail: info@bookleafpub.com

ISBN: 9789357447324

First edition 2022

DEDICATION

To everyone I love.

I think I cant think

I think I can't think.

My mind is a room,
spring is around the corner
and I have lost my broom.

Bugs and dust in my ears
cobwebs in my nostrils
imagine what my brain is
if my skull is the fossil.

Im drowning in my cortex
a hollow point is my shell
my cerebral formed a vortex
and melted away the cells.

My skeleton is the armour
red and white the link.
A matter which once was,
is no longer pink.

I think I can't think.

Dirt to Earth

Seeds are sprout which form our flowers
hoping to expand.
The fruits sit tall
some ripe some sour
but always back to land.

As time moves forward
in all its calamity.
Our bones will lower
from all of the gravity

and over time we'll melt away
like dye on a shirt.
Like rain to the water
we're dirt to the Earth.

Faces

A canvas of expression is only the face.
Sides we hide, disguised and fake.
A naked plate, no need for clothes.
Yet bare and bold when left exposed.
A mask we wear to protect the flesh.
Only suffocates us to death.

Let Go

How can I let go of what I'm stuck to?
Ties turned to knots that I can't undue.
You rubbed off on me and I on you.
In ways that we cannot remove.
Stains we cannot remove.
What remains are the remains
painted purple black and blue
the pain still remains and I do too.
Why cant I let go of you?

K.JO

I have forgotten.
The past is vague
and my memory is rotten.
The root of our fruits have gone from our youth.
Our paths cannot cross like the sun and the
moon.
But when twilight dawns at evening hours
I sit in thought and wait for you.

…

It's then when I see your star in the sky.
It's then when I find myself wondering why.
Cause those are the times your spirit's alive.
Those are the times my eyes run dry.
And when it's time, your spirit shows,
with the clouds the heavens close.
And once again
I'm left alone.

Winter & Fall

I can remember the nights
where in the dead of such a bitter world
I found warmth.

I can remember the way we fell.
How it felt.

I will never forget how beautiful the Fall had
been.
like auburn leaves from Autumn trees.

…

But I have landed now
and that was the past.
The snow has melted,
The buds have sprout
and both this Earth and I
have gone through our time of Winter.

Reflections

Im starring in the mirror again.

Disappearing,

feeling the feelings of inferior interfering with
my emotional perseverances.

Still mysterious

with too much to say from experience.

Way too serious.

A spiritual spirit who's spirit is
both well rounded and well grounded

At most spherically.

Birds & The Bees

There is nothing like love between birds and the
bees.
Flow free in the wind
like the cuffs on our sleeves.
Through every flower they pollinate,
from bud to bud they populate.
And when it seems that nature took its course,
as nature always does.
Keep in mind, the sounds of song are just a
chirp and *buzz*

Thunder & Sun

The saccharine scent of precipitations petrichor
filled the cedar forest like Christmas day cider.
A cascade of raindrops fell from out the sky
and weaved their way through branches like
highly skilled spiders.
Sounds of crackling oak and smells of soaking
soil
accompanied the thunder and aromas of natural
oils.
Mushrooms and moss grew, never few
all covered in sauce the Earth spewed, called
dew.
When the milky grey clouds cleared and all was
moist,
the heavens called out a euphonious voice.
Macaws, Cockatoos, and Finches flew
all to sing notes of nature's tune.

?

What happened to the innocence I had once
embodied?
The passion I had once sought to obtain?
What happened to the selfless love I had once so
generously given?
What happened to my imagination, my
creativity, my individualism. Where did it all
go?
Where did I go?

..

Is my identity lost in those around me?
Have I allowed this cancer we know too well as
the "social influenza" to poison my ingenuity?
Am I but a lost gene?
Have I no genesis?
I have fallen asleep.
I must wake up from this corrupt illusion.
God, please come back to me. I have gone astray
and am lost in this lie we call life. Help me wake
up so I can dream again.

Clockwork

Free to imagine.
Slave to clock-smiths and watches.
Limited by time.

Me

I saw unfamiliar faces in the most familiar
places.
Women and men, so many colours and races.
I am tired.
I cannot pretend much longer and yes, the things
that did not kill me really only made me
stronger.
Only now that it's all said and done and I have
nowhere else to run.
I learned to accept that in life you can't always
predict the outcome.
Time is of no concern at moments like these.
All that matters is me
and the man staring back.

Solitary

Confide and find confidence.
Hide and seek yourself.
Reside in self consciousness
for you and no one else.
Alone is a home and house kept quiet
where solitary walls
bring more than confinement.

One way Love

Our love is a journey and it's only one-way.
While I slept you worked tirelessly, even on
Sundays.
Gave me life while I took life away,
its only give and take, the love is one-way.
Shared wisdom to my ears
before I could talk.
Held me in your arms
Before I could walk.
No matter how I love back
as full and as best
You'll always love me more
and I'll always love you less.
One-way, no U-turns allowed.
I hope some day
I can turn it around.

Love lost

When will I find the one to share my romance.
Hold hands under setting suns and slow dance.
When will I find the one to share my soul with.
Share light and dark days as long as the solstice.
Hopeless is what I guess I've become
I just hope one day
I'll know when she comes.

Us

Acceptance is not enough and it will never be.
We fail to remember that to accept is not to love.
We seem to always want to help others,
to be the saviour of the broken
but we so often forget that we are incapable and
just as damaged.
It is more than just to accept who we are.
It is to love who, what, how, and why.
It is to love every follicle, every cell, and
molecule.
It is to embrace our disappointments and admire
our failures.
Until we have learned to become in sync with
the vibrations of our atoms will we truly love
ourselves.
We are all connected and until we know
ourselves, will we ever know each other.

Ignorance is bliss

We are oblivious to the bliss of our ignorance.

We live on it but do not live in it.
We repost but don't reform.
Like and comment but don't like to comment.
Opinionated but not open minded.

a destructive paradox to our own constructs.

Mother Nature

It is nights like these where I become the breeze,
where I embrace nature and wonder of all these
things.
The leaves and their colours greens,
the sky and its mustered navies,
the planets sitting high all in align.
The perfect sew between sows
and time before times.
As crystal and clear
and as old as wine.
I've embodied Earth
so the Earth is my body
Which only concludes that the universe is my
mind.
This is something that I know,
every star high and far represents a soul
and like seed to an oak
or an egg to a yolk
we must grow.

Because it's only mothers nature.
God is the father and Earth
Mother nature.